Sparkle- Goes to Boston

D1483397

FIREHOUSE DOG PUBLISHING, LLC®

BY FIREFIGHTER
DAYNA HILTON

Love,
Sparkles

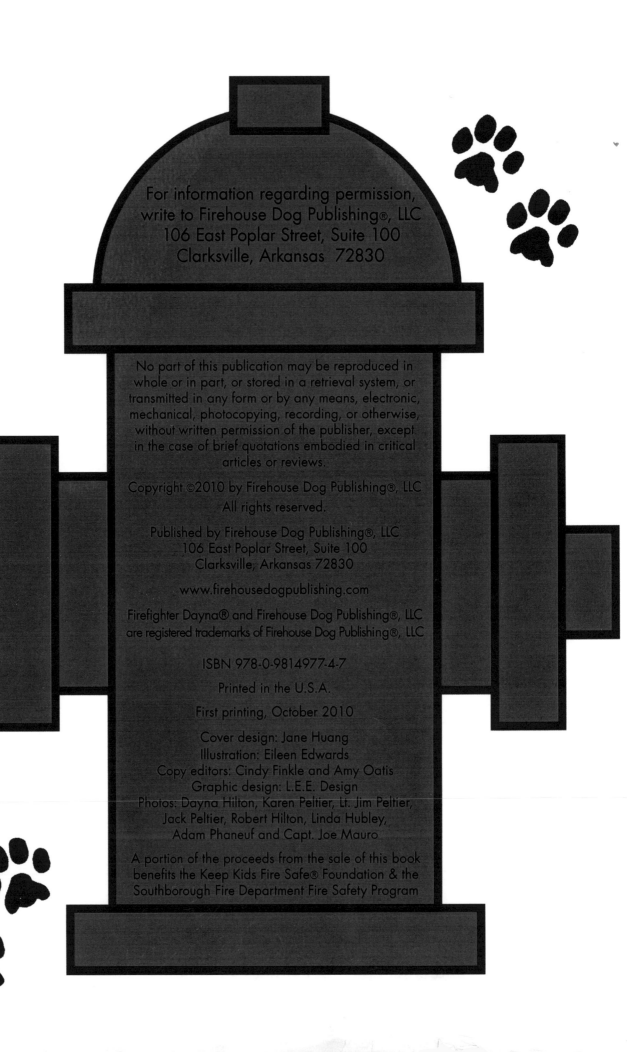

For information regarding permission,
write to Firehouse Dog Publishing®, LLC
106 East Poplar Street, Suite 100
Clarksville, Arkansas 72830

Published by Firehouse Dog Publishing®, LLC
106 East Poplar Street, Suite 100
Clarksville, Arkansas 72830

www.firehousedogpublishing.com

Firefighter Dayna® and Firehouse Dog Publishing®, LLC
are registered trademarks of Firehouse Dog Publishing®, LLC

ISBN 978-0-9814977-4-7

Printed in the U.S.A.

First printing, October 2010

Cover design: Jane Huang
Illustration: Eileen Edwards
Copy editors: Cindy Finkle and Amy Oatis
Graphic design: L.E.E. Design
Photos: Dayna Hilton, Karen Peltier, Lt. Jim Peltier,
Jack Peltier, Robert Hilton, Linda Hubley,
Adam Phaneuf and Capt. Joe Mauro

A portion of the proceeds from the sale of this book
benefits the Keep Kids Fire Safe® Foundation & the
Southborough Fire Department Fire Safety Program

Dedication

This book is dedicated to the person responsible for its inspiration: Lt. Jim Peltier with the Southborough (MA) Fire Department.

In addition, there are some very special people that I wish to thank as well. First, and foremost, to Steven Peltier, for his belief in all things related to firefighting. And to his sister, Sara, for all the times that she has made me smile. I just love your energy and creativity! And to Shawn, you are one special little boy! I will never forget the day you and Sparkles met for the first time. It was truly a special day!

Thank you to Karen Peltier for all of your support during this project. I truly appreciate everything that you and your family have done, Karen, to help make this book possible. You are an amazing family!

To my good friends Jim Peltier, Jack Peltier, and Dr. Harry Carter; I appreciate the wisdom you have imparted to me. Thank you to my husband, Robert Hilton, my son, Michael Post, Sue Peltier, Linda Hubley, Chief John Mauro, Captain Joe Mauro, Firefighter Dana Amendola, Firefighter Paul Pierce, Firefighter Tom Hogan and Firefighter Ken Franks, and the firefighters of Southborough Fire Department.

A special thank you to Jane Huang for donating your time and talents on the graphic design work for the cover and to Eileen Edwards for the illustrations on the Sparkles Goes to Boston map. Jane and Eileen, I am truly grateful to you both for helping our cause.

Lastly, I wish to thank the town of Southborough for your kindness and support during this project.

Dayna Hilton

Sparkles is excited! She cannot wait
to go with Firefighter Dayna to visit
their friends in Massachusetts.
It is a long way from Arkansas
where Sparkles lives. She is looking
forward to seeing her old friends
there and meeting new ones!

Firefighter Dayna and Sparkles
arrive at Firefighter Jim's firehouse
just on the edge of Boston.
"We're here, Sparkles!"
says Firefighter Dayna

Firefighter Jim meets them at the door.
"Hello, Sparkles! Welcome to
Southborough Fire Department."

Sparkles is extremely happy to see Firefighter Jim and wags her tail.

"Sparkles, we have some very exciting things for you to do at our firehouse," says Firefighter Jim.

"First, let's meet the Fire Chief."

"Welcome to our firehouse, Sparkles!"
says Chief Mauro. "We are
pleased that you are here!"

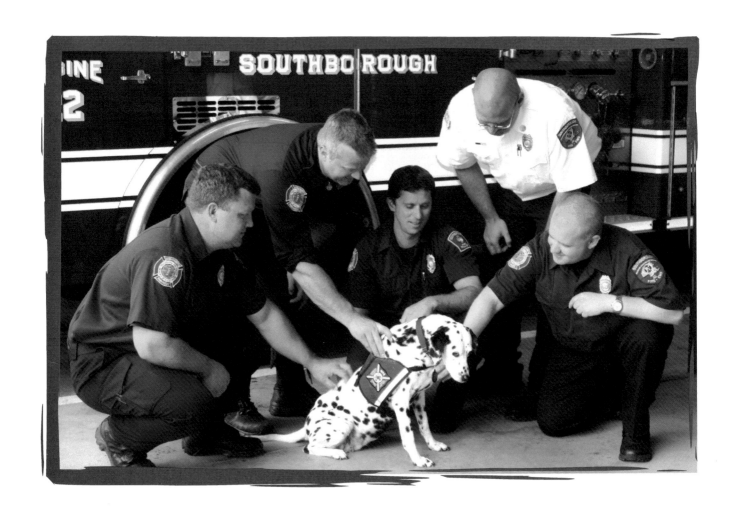

Next, Sparkles meets all the firefighters on duty. Tom, Paul, Ken and Dana come out to say hello.

Firefighter Jim wants to show
Sparkles the fire trucks.
Sparkles can't wait to see them all!

Ladder Truck

Engine

See all the big red fire trucks at
Firefighter Jim's firehouse?
The firefighters use these
trucks when there is a fire.

Brush Truck

Rescue Truck

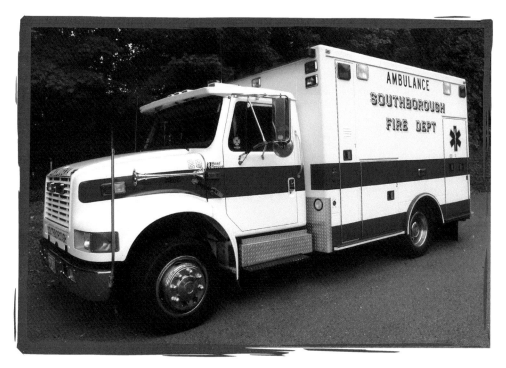

Ambulance

After seeing the fire trucks, Firefighter Jim shows Sparkles where the firefighters keep their special clothes. Firefighters wear these clothes when fighting fires. Firefighter Jim says, "This gear helps keep firefighters safe. Right, Sparkles?"

Do you see Firefighter Jim sliding down the pole? This is how firefighters get to their fire trucks quickly.

"Would you like to see where we sleep at the firehouse?" Sparkles barks and wags her tail. "Let's go upstairs!" says Firefighter Jim.

Firefighters work all day at the
firehouse. At night, firefighters need
to sleep. "Sparkles, this is where our
firefighters sleep," Firefighter Jim says.
"Now, let's go see the kitchen."

"This is the kitchen, where the firefighters eat," says Firefighter Jim. "It's lunchtime, Sparkles. Are you hungry?" The firefighters have a special bowl of dog food just for her.

Sparkles enjoys eating
lunch with the firefighters!

"Would you like to visit the school
children and help us teach fire safety,
Sparkles?" asks Firefighter Jim.
Sparkles can hardly wait! She hops
in Firefighter Jim's big red ladder truck.
Do you see the ladder?

Firefighter Jim shows the children the special firefighter clothes that help keep him safe when fighting fires.

The children take turns trying on
Firefighter Jim's gloves.
The gloves are thick.

The helmet is hard and heavy.

Firefighter Dayna asks, "Do you know how to get out of your home in case of fire?" Sparkles is excited to see the children's hands go up into the air. It is important to have an escape map and to practice home fire drills.

"If you see smoke in your home, you must get out quickly. Crawl on your hands and knees where the air is cleaner and cooler," Firefighter Dayna tells the children. She asks Sparkles to show the boys and girls how to crawl low.

Sparkles shows the children how to crawl low. Firefighter Dayna asks Steven and Sara to follow Sparkles and practice crawling low on their hands and knees.

After sharing important fire safety
tips, it is time to go. "Bye, boys
and girls. Remember to practice fire
safety every day!" say Firefighter Jim
and Firefighter Dayna.

Sparkles gets back into the
fire truck and rides to the
firehouse with Firefighter Jim.

Sparkles had such a fun and
exciting day! Now it is time to rest.
The firefighters have a special bed at
the firehouse for Sparkles.

The next morning it is time to go home to Arkansas. "Bye, Sparkles! Bye, Dayna!" the firefighters shout.

Sparkles barks and wags her tail. She will never forget what a fun time she had with her friends at the Southborough Fire Department!

The End

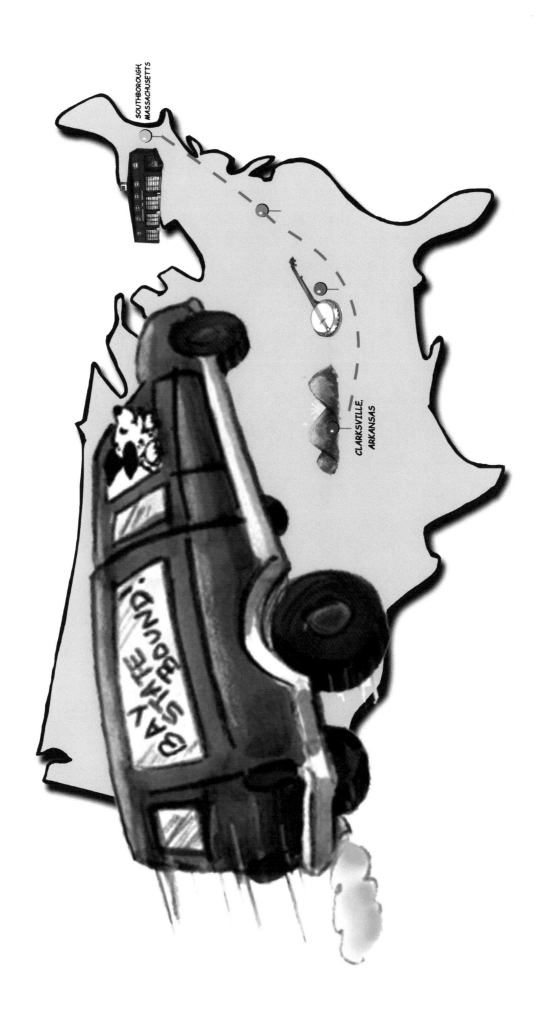

SOUTHBOROUGH, MASSACHUSETTS

CLARKSVILLE, ARKANSAS

BAY STATE BOUND!

Sparkles' Fire Safety Tips

- Recognize the firefighter as a helper and a friend.

- Stay away from hot things that hurt.

- Cool a burn with cool water.

- Tell a grown-up when you find matches or a lighter. Never touch!

- Stop, drop, and roll if your clothes catch fire.

- Know the sound and purpose of a smoke alarm.

- Practice a home fire drill using your escape map.

- Crawl low under smoke.

Tips from Oklahoma State University's Fire Protection Publications' *Fire Safety for Young Children, an Early Childhood Education Curriculum*

SPARKLES' FAVORITE LINKS

Sparkles' fire safety webpage:
www.sparklesthefiresafetydog.com

Sparkles' blog:
www.sparklesthefiresafetydog.blogspot.com

Author Firefighter Dayna Hilton's blog:
www.childrensbookauthordaynahilton.blogspot.com

Firefighter Dayna's fire safety webpage:
www.firefighterdayna.com

PBS KIDS Sprout Fire Safety Page
www.sproutonline.com/firesafety

Firehouse Dog Publishing, LLC®
www.firehousedogpublishing.com

Keep Kids Fire Safe® Foundation
www.keepkidsfiresafe.org

Southborough Fire Department
www.southboroughfire.org

Find Sparkles the Fire Safety Dog on:

Sparkles the Fire Safety Dog

"We love you, Sparkles!" has been echoed by thousands of young children since Sparkles became a fire safety dog in May 2003.

Firefighter Dayna Hilton and her family adopted Sparkles from the Dalmatian Assistance League in Tulsa, Oklahoma. Previously, Sparkles led a challenging life; she was rescued from a home with 62 other dogs. Subsequently, she has become an invaluable member of the fire service.

Sparkles has helped spread the fire safety message through her fire department, Johnson County RFD #1, and Keep Kids Fire Safe® Foundation, reaching millions of children and their caregivers. Sparkles has assisted the department's firefighters and the foundation with hundreds of fire safety programs on the local and national levels. She has come a long way since her days before adoption. Some of her most pleasurable experiences have been participating in a Congressional briefing in Washington, DC, appearing on *PBS KIDS Sprout* and *FOX and Friends* in New York City as well as having her photo appear on a jumbotron on Times Square.

Sparkles is the star of her own critically acclaimed and award-winning children's fire safety book and audio book, *Sparkles the Fire Safety Dog*. She and the book have been credited with helping save the lives of two children and their two families. In 2009, Sparkles and her book were mentioned during a Senate Homeland Security and Governmental Affairs Committee Community Preparedness Sub-Committee meeting and on the floor of Congress in Washington, DC.

Sparkles has been featured in *Cesar's Way Magazine*, *FIDO Friendly Magazine*, *DogSport Magazine*, *Tulsa Pet Magazine* and her photo appeared on the cover of the *Chicago Pet Directory* cover.

Sparkles is busy dog, sharing the message of fire safety on her website, blog, twitter and Facebook® page.

Keep Kids Fire Safe® Foundation

Five year old Angelica shared her story with me, after a fire safety event sponsored by the Rotary Club of Tulsa. "Firefighter Dayna," Angelica said, "I was in bed under the 'cobers' [covers] and the smoke came. I crawled out of bed and crawled low, just like Sparkles [the Fire Safety Dog] showed me to. I said, 'C'mon daddy, you have to get on the floor and crawl low like Sparkles.'"

By this time, her dad was disoriented because he had been standing in the smoke filled room. Fortunately, he was able to follow Angelica out of the house. Later, the firefighters shared with me that Angelica's father followed her out of the home and as soon as he reached the door, they scooped him up and took him to the hospital (where he spent 7 days~ 4 in ICU). The firefighters added that immediately after they carried him away from the front door, the home flashed over (a "flashover" is where the home becomes totally engulfed in flames).

A day does not go by where I don't think of Angelica and her story and I am so thankful that she and her dad are safe.

For almost a decade, we have concentrated our fire safety efforts on children in pre- and elementary schools.
The Keep Kids Fire Safe® Foundation is a continuation of our efforts of helping save lives, reduce injuries and decrease property loss from fire. Our goal is to develop and distribute educationally sound, innovative fire safety related materials through the foundation at little or no cost to children and their caregivers, fire departments, schools and other organizations.

The Board of Directors of the Keep Kids Fire Safe® Foundation, our benefactors, Sparkles and I do what we can to help keep children, like Angelica, fire safe.

Please consider a donation to the foundation so that together, we can help keep children and their caregivers fire safe. Visit the Keep Kids Fire Safe® Foundation website at www.keepkidsfiresafe.org to learn more.

Stay safe,

Dayna Hilton

Share your success story!

Do you have a fire safety success story? If so, we want to hear from you!

Do you know a child whose fire safety knowledge has been put to the test? Did a child you know use Sparkles the Fire Safety Dog material to help save lives during a fire-related situation? Sparkles has a special certificate to celebrate documented success stories!

Submit your story to Sparkles at:

www.sparklesthefiresafetydog.com/save_form.html

Once the success form is submitted and validated, a special certificate from Sparkles the Fire Safety Dog will be issued. Success stories will be posted on Sparkles the Fire Safety Dog's website.

This is to certify that

_____
(your name here)

is hereby granted the title of

Junior Firefighter

Practice fire safety every day!

Love, Sparkles

Sparkles the Fire Safety Dog

Acknowledgements

Cindy Finkle • Nancy Trench
Oklahoma State University Fire Protection Publications
Linda Hubley • Emily McGlaughlin
Matthew Amendola • Christopher Bigelow
Hannah Bigelow • Jimmy Bigelow • Ethan Colley
Jonathan Colley • Jerod and Blaine Colley
Ashley Phaneuf • Kelsie Phaneuf • Shea Phaneuf
Jack Tommaney • John and Lisa Tommaney
Lee and Mary White • Tim O'Dowd • Barbara Techel
Amy Oatis • Michelle Brownlow • Jessica Dockter
Clarksville Primary School • Steve Ziegler
Mrs. Kelli Grisby and the 2009/2010 Kindergarten Class

Southborough Fire Department

The Southborough Fire Department is a combination department staffed by a minimum of four full-time Firefighter/EMTs, augmented by an on-call force, operating one fire station.

Members of the department provide fire, rescue and emergency medical response as well as inspection, prevention and public education programs to just over 10,000 residents in a 13.78 square mile area. Included in the department's first-due response area are two interstate highways (I-90 & I-495), three state highways Routes 9, 30 & 85), two CSX rail lines (including the MBTA commuter rail Worcester line), two private boarding schools (Fay & St. Mark's), the New England Center for Children, as well as Harvard University's New England Regional Primate Research Center and Book Depository. A large EMC Campus, as well as several commercial, industrial, and office properties are located along Route 9.

Mission Statement

It is the mission of the Members of the Southborough Fire Department to provide the highest level of service and professionalism to the Community. We, as a united team, shall respond to a wide variety of Fire, Rescue and Emergency calls in a timely manner. The image of a dedicated, skilled, honest, proud, loyal and cohesive group is a common thread in all the members.

it is also our mission to minimize and prevent fire from occurring through fire prevention and public education, and to come to the aid of the sick and injured by responding with certified EMT's and Paramedics, and by serving as a community resource by offering CPR and First Responder training. Also, participating within the community in a wide variety of activities.

Thank you to PJ Phaneuf and his family for the use of
"Danvers Engine 4" for the cover of *Sparkles Goes to Boston*.

Danvers Engine 4 is a 1936 Peter Pirsch 600 GPM pumper. It served
Danvers from 1936 until the mid 1960's. At that time, it was sold to
the Moose River Maine Fire Department and was used as a water tender.

The Phaneuf's have owned the engine since the late 1980's.
Peter F. Phaneuf is a Retired Southborough Fire Chief with 47 years
of service. Peter (PJ) is a Firefighter/Paramedic and he currently
serves as the Training Coordinator for the Foxborough (MA) Fire
Department. Adam Phaneuf, Peter's brother, was a call firefighter
with the Southborough Fire Department.

Other Items from Firehouse Dog Publishing®

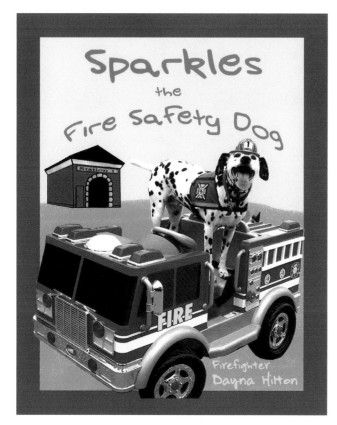

Sparkles the Fire Safety Dog
2nd Edition
ISBN: 978-0-9814977-3-0

Critically acclaimed, award-winning children's fire safety book, *Sparkles the Fire Safety Dog*, by Firefighter Dayna Hilton.

Inspired by her work as a firefighter and her four-legged friend, Sparkles, author Firefighter Dayna Hilton created a heart-warming story about Sparkles.

As children learn of the adventures of Sparkles the Fire Safety Dog, they learn valuable fire safety tips enabling them and their families to help keep fire safe. These tips include recognizing the firefighter as a helper and a friend, knowing the sound and purpose of a smoke alarm, learning how to crawl low under smoke, and understanding the importance of practicing a home fire drill using an escape map. *Sparkles the Fire Safety Dog* is not only fun, but educationally sound and based on the latest fire safety research for young children.

A portion of all book proceeds from *Sparkles the Fire Safety Dog* will be donated to the Keep Kids Fire Safe® Foundation.

This 26-page coloring book is a perfect stand alone coloring book or companion piece to *Sparkles Goes to Boston* and *Sparkles the Fire Safety Dog*.

Join Sparkles as she achieves her dream of becoming a real fire safety dog.

Written by Firefighter Dayna Hilton with artwork by Eileen Edwards, children will delight in reading Sparkles' story.

*A portion of all book proceeds from the *Sparkles the Fire Safety Dog Coloring Book* will be donated to the Keep Kids Fire Safe® Foundation.

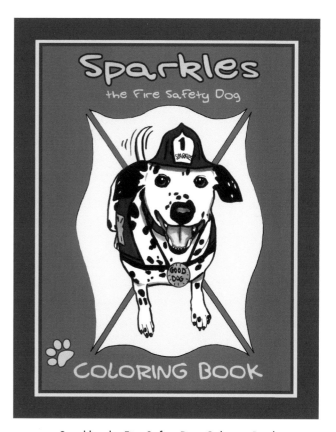

Sparkles the Fire Safety Dog Coloring Book
ISBN: 978-0-9814977-5-4

Firefighter Dayna Hilton and her fire safety dogs have made it their mission to save lives, reduce injuries, and decrease property loss from fire for almost a decade.

As a second generation firefighter, Hilton joined the fire service in August 2000 and is recognized as one of the leading fire safety educators in the country.

Hilton is founder and Executive Director of Keep Kids Fire Safe® Foundation, owner of Firehouse Dog Publishing, LLC® and the author of the award-winning, critically acclaimed children's fire safety book and audio book, *Sparkles the Fire Safety Dog.*

Hilton, along with her fire safety dogs, have appeared on *PBS KIDS Sprout* and on *FOX and Friends.*

LaVergne, TN USA
05 October 2010
199394LV00003BA